# A CHILD'S STORY OF THANKSGIVING

By *Laura J. Rader*
*Illustrated by*
Mary Ann Utt

Ideals Children's Books • Nashville, Tennessee
an imprint of Hambleton-Hill Publishing, Inc.

*To Mama, and in memory of Grandma, who taught me to love reading and books.*
*—L.J.R.*
*To Mom and Dad*
*—M.A.U.*

Text copyright © 1998 by Hambleton-Hill Publishing, Inc.
Illustrations copyright © 1998 by Hambleton-Hill Publishing, Inc.

ING 11/10/99 6.95L

Published by Ideals Children's Books
An imprint of Hambleton-Hill Publishing, Inc.
Nashville, Tennessee 37218

**Library of Congress Cataloging-in-Publication Data**
Rader, Laura.
   A child's story of Thanksgiving / by Laura Rader ; illustrated by Mary Ann
Utt. — 1st ed.
     p.   cm.
   Summary: Briefly chronicles Thanksgiving celebrations from fifteenth
century Massachusetts to the present.
   ISBN 1-57102-134-5 (hardcover)
   1. Thanksgiving Day—Juvenile literature. [1. Thanksgiving Day.]
I. Utt, Mary Ann.  II. Title.
   GT4975.R33   1998
    394.2649—dc21                         98-16611
                                         CIP
                                         AC

The illustrations in this book were rendered in watercolor and colored pencil.
The text type is set in Sabon.
The display type is set in Goudy and Nuptial Script.

First Edition

10 9 8 7 6 5 4 3 2 1

Almost everyone thinks of turkey, cranberry sauce, and pumpkin pie at Thanksgiving. They are important parts of a traditional Thanksgiving celebration. But Thanksgiving is about more than just eating a big meal.

A long time ago, King James I of England said that everyone had to join the same church or leave the country. A group of people called Puritans would not do this; they wanted to be able to worship God the way they wanted to.

Because of this, a lot of Puritans were put in prison, and some were even hanged. Finally, a group of these people snuck out of England and moved to Holland.

The Puritans were not happy living in Holland. They were used to country living and farming in England, and there was not enough land for farming in Holland. They wanted to try to make a life for themselves in America. Their group was too small, however, so they got some other people who wanted to go with them.

Finally a group of 102 men, women, and children set sail for America on a ship called the *Mayflower*. The entire group of people who came on that ship came to be called Pilgrims, which means "religious wanderers."

The journey was a very difficult one. There were lots of storms, and the Pilgrims were very scared. They had to stay below deck, and the rocking of the ship made many of them seasick. Finally, after two months at sea, they first saw land.

Though this was not where they had originally planned to go, the Pilgrims decided to make this place, Massachusetts, their new home rather than keep travelling on the stormy ocean. On December 11, 1620, the Pilgrims landed on Plymouth Harbor beach.

The winter at this place was very hard. It was so cold that the men were not able to get houses built. The Pilgrims had to stay on the ship. They were running out of the food that they had brought with them from England.

And because it was too late in the year to plant crops, and because they didn't know how to hunt or fish very well, it was very difficult to get more. The Pilgrims grew weak from hunger, and they began to get sick. Many of them died. When spring arrived, only fifty-seven of the Pilgrims and half of the Mayflower crew had survived.

The following
spring, the surviving
Pilgrims planted seeds.
The types of crops they
had grown as farmers in England did not grow well in this New Land. A
Native American named Squanto, whose village had once been nearby,
noticed this. He showed the Pilgrims how to plant corn, squash, beans, and
pumpkins, which they had never grown before.

He also showed the Pilgrims the best places to catch fish and the best ways to catch them. He took the men hunting; he showed the children where to pick wild strawberries, cranberries, and gooseberries. Because of Squanto's help, that year's harvest produced more food than the Pilgrims thought possible.

Back in England, it was customary to mark the end of the harvest with a big festival. The Pilgrims also wanted to give thanks to God for helping them survive the long journey from England and the hard winter. So they planned a big celebration with food and games for everyone in the community. The Pilgrims invited their friend Squanto, who had done so much to help them have a good harvest. They asked him to bring some other Native Americans to the celebration.

Four married ladies who were really good cooks were chosen to prepare the meal. The men set barrels in the middle of the only street in Plymouth. They set boards on the barrels and covered the boards with fine linen cloths. They also hunted the turkeys and ducks that the women cooked. Young women and children helped to do many things. They gathered berries, chopped vegetables, brought water, and gathered wood for fires to cook the food.

The meal probably included roasted deer meat; turkeys stuffed with nuts and dried fruits; boiled pumpkin (there was no flour or molassses to make pies with); corn, which was made into a type of cornbread; cranberries, which were probably boiled to make a sauce; and fish and seafood such as eel and lobster.

Celebration day came and Squanto arrived, bringing ninety guests with him. The women were surprised; they had only made enough food for sixty people! The Native Americans had brought deer and many turkeys to contribute to the feast. The women cooked these and began making more food so that there would be enough for everyone.

They must have succeeded, because the celebration lasted for three days. Everyone ate, played games, sang, and danced.

People today do many of those same things when celebrating Thanksgiving. They get together with their families; they invite friends to celebrate with them. Usually there is a big meal with many of the same kinds of food the Pilgrims ate on the first Thanksgiving: turkey with stuffing, sweet potatoes, cranberries (made into sauce) and pumpkins (baked into pumpkin pies!) Football is probably the most popular game for Thanksgiving today. People often gather to watch their favorite teams play. Some people like to play an informal game of touch football.

Because Thanksgiving is a time of sharing, it is often customary to share not just with friends and family, but with strangers who may be poor and hungry.

Volunteering to help at homeless shelters is a way many people spend Thanksgiving. For them, giving to others is a way to show thanks for all that they themselves have been given.

Every fall at Thanksgiving, people discover that there are almost as many ways to celebrate and show thanks as there are things to be thankful for. Just as the Pilgrims did, people take time to remember and give thanks for the blessings they have received.